MARKETING KARMA

THE ENLIGHTENED PATH TO DIGITAL SUCCESS

JAYADEV K T

INDIA • SINGAPORE • MALAYSIA

Copyright © Jayadev K T 2023
All Rights Reserved.

ISBN 979-8-89066-923-0

This book has been published with all efforts taken to make the material error-free after the consent of the author. However, the author and the publisher do not assume and hereby disclaim any liability to any party for any loss, damage, or disruption caused by errors or omissions, whether such errors or omissions result from negligence, accident, or any other cause.

While every effort has been made to avoid any mistake or omission, this publication is being sold on the condition and understanding that neither the author nor the publishers or printers would be liable in any manner to any person by reason of any mistake or omission in this publication or for any action taken or omitted to be taken or advice rendered or accepted on the basis of this work. For any defect in printing or binding the publishers will be liable only to replace the defective copy by another copy of this work then available.

CONTENTS

Preface: A Spiritual Introduction to Marketing 7

Chapter 1   **The Nature of Existence and Marketing** 11

     1.1 Life's Imperative: Marketing in Nature 12
     1.2 The Principle of Attraction: Marketing and Evolution 13
     1.3 The Marketing Universe: Creating Cosmic Connections 14

Chapter 2   **The Wheel of Digital Dharma** 19

     2.1 The Ethical Guidelines for Marketing 21
     2.2 The Balance of Needs: The Marketer, The Marketed, and The Market 21
     2.3 Karma in Marketing: The Law of Cause and Effect 22

Chapter 3   **Understanding the Modern Marketplace: The World Wide Web** 27

     3.1 Spiritual Analogy of the Internet 29
     3.2 Mindfulness in the Digital Crowd 29
     3.3 The Search for Truth: SEO as a Path 30

Chapter 4   **Social Media and the Consciousness of Connection** 35

     4.1 The Social Mandala: Navigating Digital Relationships 37
     4.2 Beyond the Illusion: Real Impact in Virtual Platforms 37
     4.3 Authenticity in Social Media: The Practice of Satya 38

• Contents •

Chapter 5   **Content Creation: The Digital Sutra** 43

    5.1 Storytelling as Sacred Ritual 44
    5.2 The Power of Resonance: Frequency and Virality 44
    5.3 Content Altruism: Sharing as a Form of Giving 45

Chapter 6   **Customer Engagement: The Dance of Interaction** 49

    6.1 Mindful Listening: The Art of Customer Response 50
    6.2 Serving as a Digital Yogi: Customer Service with Compassion 50
    6.3 Constructive Conversations: Moving Beyond Negative Feedback 51

Chapter 7   **Data and Analytics: The Insight Meditation** 55

    7.1 Data: The Divine Mirror 56
    7.2 Wisdom in Numbers: Interpreting Analytics 56
    7.3 Forecasting: The Power of Predictive Insight 57

Chapter 8   **Evolving through the Eras: From Traditional to Digital Marketing** 61

    8.1 The Shift: Transformation towards New Media 62
    8.2 Lessons from the Past: Holding onto Ethical Roots 62
    8.3 Embracing Change: The Impermanence of Marketing Trends 63

Chapter 9   **Brand Karma: Sowing the Seeds for Long Term Success** 67

    9.1 The Ethics of Branding: Truthfulness and Transparency 68
    9.2 Cultivating a Conscious Brand: Social Responsibility and Sustainability 68

• Contents •

9.3 The Brand Life Cycle: Birth, Growth, Transformation, Rebirth..69

Chapter 10 Marketing Nirvana: Creating Enlightened Campaigns 73

10.1 Defining Success: Profits and Purpose...............................74
10.2 Beyond ROI: The Holistic Impact of Marketing...............74
10.3 Manifesting Abundance: A Path to Sustainable Success.....75

*Afterword: The Journey Continues: Marketing as a
Path to Enlightenment* *79*

Appendices *83*

Appendix A: Marketing Mantras for Daily Practice....................... *83*
Appendix B: Marketing Ethics Code *85*
Appendix C: Suggested Reading and Resources............................... *86*

Glossary of Terms *87*

PREFACE: A SPIRITUAL INTRODUCTION TO MARKETING

Marketing is not often viewed through the lens of spirituality. After all, marketing is often seen as an aggressive, profit-centric activity, steeped in competition and at times, manipulation. Spirituality, on the other hand, is associated with peace, harmony, and a focus on higher truths beyond the material world. These two domains appear to exist in separate realities, like oil and water refusing to mix.

However, when we pause to contemplate, we realize that spirituality and marketing share a common heart - the art of communication, the practice of connection. In spirituality, we strive to understand and articulate the mysteries of life, to establish a relationship with the divine, and communicate the joy of such unity to others. In marketing, we aim to understand the core of a product or service and then connect that essence with the individuals who will benefit from it.

At its core, marketing is about fulfilling needs, spreading awareness, and fostering connections. It is about discerning a vacuum and aiming to fill it with value. Isn't that what spirituality also endeavors? Spirituality helps us recognize our internal voids - be it peace, joy, or a sense of purpose - and guides us to fill these gaps with higher wisdom and divine love.

In this book, we aim to bridge the apparent gap between these two fields, presenting an enlightened approach to marketing. Here, we consider marketing not just as a tool for business enhancement but as an integral part of the human experience. We delve into the spiritual principles that have a natural place in the world of marketing. Principles like Karma, the cause-effect relation reflected in customer response; Dharma, the ethical path every marketer should tread; Satya, the practice of truthfulness in communicating your message, and many more.

Just as spirituality is a journey toward self-understanding and transcendence, marketing can be viewed as a journey toward understanding others' needs and creating value that transcends mere transactions. When we perceive marketing as a spiritual practice, it transforms from a chore or a challenge into a meaningful path of service. It becomes less about selling and more about sharing; less about revenue and more about resonance; less about competition and more about compassion.

In essence, the purpose of this book is to inspire and guide marketers to practice their profession with a higher consciousness. Through a spiritual lens, we invite you to view marketing not just as a strategy for business growth, but as a platform for positive change, a tool for mutual benefit, and a path towards a more connected, compassionate, and conscious world.

As we embark on this journey, remember, spirituality doesn't demand us to renounce our roles in the marketplace; instead, it provides us the wisdom to play them better, with a sense of service and love. So let's commence this enlightening journey of 'Marketing Karma,' understanding and implementing digital marketing principles with a spiritual twist.

One of the key elements of this book is the self-assessment section at the end of each chapter. These assessments serve as a reflection tool to gauge your understanding of the content and apply the insights you've gained to your own life or work.

Preface: A Spiritual Introduction to Marketing

Each self-assessment contains a set of carefully designed questions intended to stimulate your thought processes and encourage introspection. The goal is not to 'pass' or 'fail', but to gauge where you stand regarding the principles and ideas discussed in the chapter. The answers are deeply personal and subjective, hence there are no right or wrong responses.

Each question is designed to help you contemplate your current practices and mindsets. Are they aligned with the enlightened marketing path we're exploring? Are there areas where you're strong, and areas where you could grow?

The beauty of these assessments is that they can be taken multiple times. As you progress through your spiritual marketing journey, you may find your responses evolving. This evolution is a sign of growth and learning. So, keep revisiting these assessments as you move forward.

By introspecting and being honest with your responses, you'll gain a clearer vision of your current approach and a roadmap for your journey towards marketing nirvana. Remember, the journey of self-improvement is ongoing and these self-assessments are here to guide and support you in this endeavor.

May each question bring you closer to enlightenment, and may your insights be the beacon that guides you on the path of conscious and purpose-driven marketing.

CHAPTER 1

THE NATURE OF EXISTENCE AND MARKETING

"The dance of nature echoes in every marketing interaction; it's a rhythmic call-and-response, a timeless exchange of value."

Imagine a garden, a microcosm of life, teeming with various forms of existence. The flowers bloom with radiant colors and fragrances, inviting the bees with their sweet nectar. The bees, in turn, carry pollen from one blossom to another, playing a crucial role in the garden's growth and prosperity. This symbiosis is natural marketing at its core – a non-intrusive, mutually beneficial exchange of value.

Similarly, consider an ethical business in the global marketplace. The business cultivates a unique value proposition, much like the flower's nectar. It presents this value in an appealing manner, through engaging narratives and attractive designs. The target audience, akin to the bees, is drawn towards this value. In the process of consuming this value (buying the products or services), the audience also aids the business's growth by spreading word of their positive experiences, thus attracting more potential customers.

This exchange forms the essence of marketing in harmony with the nature of existence. It's a dance of reciprocity where every party involved contributes to and benefits from the collective wellbeing. When marketing aligns with these universal principles, it becomes an integral part of life's interconnected web, fostering healthier relationships and sustainable growth.

1.1 Life's Imperative: Marketing in Nature

Nature is the greatest marketer of all. Each organism, in its own way, markets itself for survival. The vibrant peacock unfurls its splendid plumage to attract a mate. Flowers bloom into breathtaking beauty to attract pollinators, ensuring their survival and propagation. In essence, life markets its existence, its uniqueness, its purpose.

As humans, we are an integral part of this natural marketing spectacle. We market our skills to get a job, our personality traits to create relationships, our ideas to make an impact. This act of 'marketing' ourselves, our products or services, isn't merely a business strategy. It's a fundamental aspect of life, an expression of existence.

The key to effective marketing, as observed in nature, lies in authenticity. Each entity in nature is authentic in its expression. It does not aim to be what it is not. A rose does not strive to be a lily, nor a peacock a lion. When we align our marketing strategies with this natural authenticity, recognizing and showcasing the true essence of what we offer, our messages resonate deeper and yield better results.

1.2 The Principle of Attraction: Marketing and Evolution

The principle of attraction is one of the foundational pillars of evolution, ensuring the survival and propagation of life forms. Attraction operates at all levels of existence, from particles to planets. It's this principle that draws customers towards a product or service in the world of marketing.

Consider Darwin's theory of natural selection. The creatures most adapted to their environment are the ones most likely to survive and reproduce. In the context of marketing, the offerings most adapted to the customer's needs and desires are the ones most likely to be 'selected,' leading to the 'survival' and success of the business.

By understanding and harnessing this principle of attraction, we can evolve our marketing strategies. We focus not on selling but attracting, not on convincing but connecting. Our marketing messages become like a magnetic field, drawing in those who resonate with what we have to offer.

1.3 The Marketing Universe: Creating Cosmic Connections

The universe is an intricate web of interconnections. Every star, every planet, every atom is interconnected in this cosmic dance of existence. Similarly, in the marketing universe, everything is interconnected.

Each product, each service, each brand, each customer - all are part of this interconnected marketing universe. Each action, each campaign, each interaction affects not only the immediate receiver but also the whole system.

Recognizing these interconnections can help us create holistic marketing strategies. Our actions become about more than immediate gain. We aim for mutual benefit, understanding that the success of one is linked to the success of all. We create not just transactions but relationships, not just conversions but connections.

This perspective shifts our approach from competition to cooperation, from isolation to integration. We see ourselves not as individual entities fighting for a piece of the market but as part of a greater whole, contributing to a thriving marketing cosmos.

In essence, understanding the nature of existence and marketing allows us to align our strategies with these universal principles. It infuses our marketing practice with a depth of purpose and a sense of interconnectedness, leading to authentic expression, meaningful attraction, and conscious connection.

Chapter 1: Self-Assessment Quiz

Marketing is a fundamental part of life's interconnected web. How much do you agree with this statement?

- Completely Agree
- Mostly Agree
- Neutral
- Mostly Disagree
- Completely Disagree

How would you describe the role of marketing in the ecosystem of your business?

- Solely for promotion of products or services
- For relationship building and communication
- For creating, delivering, and communicating value
- Not sure

The Principle of Attraction applies in marketing through:

- Creating visually appealing content
- Creating value for the customer
- Both A and B
- None of the above

Which best describes your understanding of marketing's role in creating cosmic connections?

- Focusing on transactional relationships with customers
- Building long-term relationships and networks
- Reaching out to as many potential customers as possible
- None of the above

Do you consider marketing as just a business process or an essential part of existence and life's functioning?

- Just a business process
- An essential part of existence and life's functioning
- Both
- None of the above

Can marketing activities influence the balance of needs between the marketer, the marketed, and the market?

- Yes
- No
- Unsure

CHAPTER 2

THE WHEEL OF DIGITAL DHARMA

"In the wheel of digital dharma, ethical marketing holds the center, stabilizing the spin of demand and supply, vision and execution."

Imagine you're a farmer, tending to your field. You begin by planting seeds in the fertile soil, each seed carrying the potential to sprout, grow, and bear fruit. However, you don't simply scatter the seeds and leave them to their fate. You water them, ensure they receive adequate sunlight, protect them from pests, and tend to their needs as they sprout and grow. Your actions reflect an understanding of the law of cause and effect, a commitment to the welfare of the seed, and a hope for a fruitful harvest.

This farming analogy can be applied to ethical marketing. The seeds you sow are your marketing efforts, the fertile soil represents the digital landscape, and the nurturing care you provide stands for the ethical guidelines adhered to in these efforts. The successful harvest is the resulting customer satisfaction and business growth.

In the digital era, the 'Wheel of Dharma' revolves faster. Every tweet, post, or email you send out is a seed sown in the field of potential customer engagement. However, how you plant these seeds, how mindfully you water and tend to them, determines the quality of the harvest.

You need to ensure your marketing respects the dignity and autonomy of the audience, upholds transparency, and provides genuine value. This is the 'Wheel of Digital Dharma,' where mindful actions lead to meaningful reactions. The resulting success is not just monetary but also the establishment of trust and relationships, the true fruits of ethical marketing.

By following the 'Wheel of Digital Dharma,' you not only create successful marketing campaigns, but you also contribute positively to the digital ecosystem, reinforcing a cycle of respect, mutual growth, and meaningful engagement.

2.1 The Ethical Guidelines for Marketing

In the world of digital marketing, where the audience's attention is constantly being sought after, ethical guidelines become a critical cornerstone. Just as the principles of Dharma govern a harmonious, righteous life, they also provide a moral compass for marketers to navigate the digital landscape.

Transparency is a fundamental ethical guideline. Digital marketers must make clear to consumers the nature of the goods or services they're offering, along with any associated costs, terms, or conditions.

Privacy is another key consideration. In an age where data can be both a tool and a weapon, it is imperative to respect and protect user privacy. Informed consent for data collection and usage should be a standard practice.

Finally, authenticity is crucial. Authenticity promotes trust and fosters long-term relationships with customers. It is essential to promote products or services truthfully, without making misleading or deceptive claims.

2.2 The Balance of Needs: The Marketer, The Marketed, and The Market

The principle of balance is crucial in the marketing universe. It calls for the harmonious alignment of the needs of the marketer, the marketed, and the market.

The marketer's needs often involve achieving business goals, such as increasing brand awareness, sales, or customer retention. The marketed, or customers, look for products or services that address their needs or wants, provide value, and improve their quality of life. The market, or society at large, needs businesses to operate responsibly, contributing positively to the community and environment.

In the spirit of Dharma, it is vital to balance these needs. A marketing strategy that only serves the marketer, neglecting the needs of customers and the wider society, is unsustainable and unethical. Conversely, a balanced marketing strategy, which considers and integrates the needs of all parties, fosters success, trust, and goodwill.

2.3 Karma in Marketing: The Law of Cause and Effect

The law of Karma - every action has a consequence - holds true even in the realm of marketing. Every marketing action, every message sent, every campaign launched creates a ripple effect. These actions can influence a brand's reputation, customer sentiment, and ultimately, its success.

Good marketing karma is born of practices that add value, foster trust, and create positive experiences for customers. Misleading advertisements, invasive practices, or unethical behavior, on the other hand, can lead to negative karma, damaging a brand's reputation and customer relationships.

Thus, it is wise for digital marketers to be mindful of the karmic consequences of their actions. In the grand scheme of things, ethical, customer-centric, and value-driven marketing practices don't just serve short-term goals; they sow the seeds of long-term success, prosperity, and positive karma.

Chapter 2: Self-Assessment Quiz

How much do you agree with the statement that ethical guidelines are integral to effective marketing?

- Completely Agree
- Mostly Agree
- Neutral
- Mostly Disagree
- Completely Disagree

Which of the following best defines your approach to maintaining balance in marketing?

- Prioritizing the needs of the business
- Prioritizing the needs of the customer
- Striving to balance the needs of the business, the customer, and the wider market
- Not sure

How would you apply the concept of 'karma' in your marketing activities?

- Focusing primarily on the immediate results of a campaign
- Recognizing the potential long-term impact of your marketing activities on the brand's reputation
- I don't see how 'karma' relates to marketing
- None of the above

In the context of digital marketing, do you believe in the principle of 'what goes around, comes around'?

- Yes
- No
- Unsure

How often do you consider ethical implications when planning a digital marketing campaign?

- Always
- Sometimes
- Rarely
- Never

Do you believe that every action in the digital marketing world, like in life, has consequences?

- Yes
- No
- Unsure

CHAPTER 3

UNDERSTANDING THE MODERN MARKETPLACE: THE WORLD WIDE WEB

"The web of connection weaves us into a single tapestry. To market is to understand the threads that connect us all."

Imagine stepping into a vast, bustling bazaar. Here, merchants from every corner of the world come to display their wares. Buyers, attracted by the range of items on offer, wander from stall to stall, exploring, examining, and eventually, making purchases that appeal to their unique needs or desires. Yet, this bazaar isn't located in any physical location. It's accessible from every corner of the world and operates round the clock. This is the World Wide Web, the modern marketplace.

A business trying to establish itself in this space is much like a new merchant setting up a stall in this global bazaar. The merchant's first task is to ensure they are discoverable amidst the crowd. This is akin to a business optimizing its online presence for search engines, making sure when customers seek products or services they offer, they find their way to them.

The merchant then needs to present their wares attractively and accurately. Similarly, a business must craft a compelling and honest narrative around its products and services, using all available digital tools like websites, social media platforms, and email campaigns.

Finally, the merchant needs to engage with the customers, answer their queries, and persuade them of the value of their wares. Analogously, businesses need to engage with their online audience, answer their questions, understand their needs, and cater to them efficiently.

Understanding the World Wide Web as the modern marketplace is vital for businesses to survive and thrive. They need to recognize its unique nature, adapt their strategies accordingly, and align their goals with the digital landscape's inherent dynamics. The journey might seem daunting at first, but with a deep understanding and mindful implementation, it transforms into an enlightening path towards growth and success.

3.1 Spiritual Analogy of the Internet

The internet can be seen as a microcosm of the universe. It reflects the interconnectedness and infinite potential that spiritual traditions have always spoken about.

In this digital cosmos, websites are akin to stars, each one unique and shining with its own light. Social media platforms are like galaxies, hosting countless stars and facilitating connections between them. Search engines like Google serve as guides, helping us navigate this vast cosmos to find the stars that resonate with our queries.

Just as our actions in the physical universe create karma, our actions in the digital universe do the same. Every post, every comment, every share creates a ripple effect. It can bring light and value to others, or it can spread darkness and misinformation. Hence, it's crucial to tread the digital path with consciousness, integrity, and responsibility.

3.2 Mindfulness in the Digital Crowd

In the crowded digital marketplace, mindfulness is a powerful tool. It allows marketers to stay present, maintain focus, and act with intention, amid the constant noise and distraction.

Mindfulness involves listening deeply to your audience. It's about understanding their needs, their challenges, their desires, and responding with empathy and relevance. It also involves being aware of the wider impact of your marketing actions on the community and environment.

In the race for attention and clicks, it's easy to lose sight of the human beings behind the screen. Mindful marketing brings the human element back into focus. It reminds us that behind every like, every share, every purchase, there's a person with hopes, dreams, and struggles.

3.3 The Search for Truth: SEO as a Path

Search Engine Optimization (SEO) is more than a technical strategy for improving website visibility. It can be viewed as a spiritual path in the quest for truth.

In the context of SEO, 'truth' refers to relevant, valuable, and authentic content that fulfills the searcher's intent. Just as a spiritual seeker strives for self-realization, an SEO marketer strives to realize the true needs and intents of their audience and address them effectively.

Practicing SEO with this perspective transforms it from a mechanical process into a meaningful practice. It's no longer just about ranking higher on search engine results pages, but about guiding searchers towards their truth - towards the answers, solutions, or experiences they seek.

Thus, the modern marketplace - the World Wide Web - becomes a digital dharma field, a platform for practicing conscious, mindful, and truthful marketing. It becomes a platform for adding value, fostering connections, and contributing to the greater good.

■ Understanding the Modern Marketplace: The World Wide Web ■

Chapter 3: Self-Assessment Quiz

The Internet can be considered a spiritual analogy for:

- Complexity and Chaos
- Interconnectedness and Unity
- Anarchy and Disorder
- None of the above

How often do you practice mindfulness when navigating the digital crowd?

- Always
- Sometimes
- Rarely
- Never

What does SEO (Search Engine Optimization) mean to you in the context of the search for truth?

- Manipulating algorithms for higher search rankings
- Creating value-driven content that meets the real needs of users
- Both A and B
- None of the above

Do you think the practice of mindfulness can improve your digital marketing activities?

- Yes
- No
- Unsure

In your opinion, what is the role of empathy in understanding the modern digital marketplace?

- Critical
- Important but not essential
- Not important
- Unsure

How do you adapt your marketing strategies to the dynamic and ever-changing nature of the Digital World?

- I consistently observe and adjust my strategies based on current trends and changes
- I set my strategies and follow them regardless of changes
- I sporadically change strategies based on major shifts in the digital landscape
- Not sure

CHAPTER 4

SOCIAL MEDIA AND THE CONSCIOUSNESS OF CONNECTION

"Through the lens of social media, we witness the interplay of thoughts and emotions, creating an orchestra of human connection."

Let's consider a huge gathering, much like the ancient 'Kumbh Mela' of India. Millions gather from all walks of life, sharing stories, experiences, and forming connections. This is the essence of social media - a global gathering of individuals and entities who are there to connect, share, and grow.

Suppose you are an ethical business venturing into this vast gathering. Much like a participant at the 'Kumbh Mela,' you carry your unique story, your purpose, and your offerings. The goal isn't to shout the loudest to be heard but to find those who resonate with your story and would benefit from your offerings.

This journey begins with authenticity. You share your story truthfully, express your purpose clearly, and present your offerings honestly. Just like the natural resonance of a bell, your authenticity attracts those who align with your purpose. This is akin to creating a genuine online presence that resonates with your target audience.

Next, you engage in meaningful conversations, you listen and you share, cultivating a genuine bond with those around you. In the realm of social media, this translates to engaging content, timely responses to comments or queries, and a genuine interest in your audience's needs and feedback.

Finally, you respect the space you are in and contribute to its positivity and growth. On social media, this means being aware of the platform's guidelines, respecting the digital space of others, contributing valuable content, and being a positive influence.

Social media, when approached with the consciousness of connection, becomes more than a marketing tool. It becomes a medium to form meaningful relationships, to learn, to grow, and to contribute positively to the global community. It becomes an embodiment of the ancient wisdom of 'Vasudhaiva Kutumbakam' - The world is one family.

4.1 The Social Mandala: Navigating Digital Relationships

The Mandala, a spiritual symbol representing the universe, can be a beautiful metaphor for understanding social media. Each platform - Facebook, Twitter, Instagram, LinkedIn, and others - are like various circles within the Mandala. These circles represent different communities, interests, conversations, and interactions, all interconnected within the grand design of the digital universe.

To effectively navigate these digital relationships, marketers must develop a deep understanding of each circle's unique characteristics, the audience it attracts, the content it resonates with. Just as a spiritual aspirant approaches a Mandala with reverence and focus, a marketer must approach each social media platform with respect for its unique culture and norms.

4.2 Beyond the Illusion: Real Impact in Virtual Platforms

While social media platforms are virtual, the impact they create is very real. They have the power to spread ideas, inspire actions, foster communities, and even influence global events. In many ways, they mirror the spiritual concept of Maya - the illusion that veils the underlying reality.

As marketers, it's crucial to look beyond the illusions - the vanity metrics, the highlight reels, the viral trends - and focus on creating real, tangible impact. This involves sharing content that educates, inspires, uplifts, adds value, and promotes positive change. It also involves engaging genuinely with your audience, fostering a sense of community, and facilitating meaningful conversations.

4.3 Authenticity in Social Media: The Practice of Satya

Satya, or truthfulness, is a fundamental spiritual principle, and it holds immense value in the realm of social media marketing. With the rise of 'fake news', misinformation, and superficiality on social media, authenticity has become a rare commodity and thus, more precious.

Practicing Satya in social media marketing involves presenting your brand, products, or services honestly. It's about owning your strengths and acknowledging your weaknesses. It's about honoring your commitments and standing by your values, even when they're not popular or trending.

When you practice Satya, your audience perceives you as trustworthy and reliable. They know they can count on you for accurate information, genuine interaction, and real value. In a landscape often clouded by falsehoods and facades, your authenticity shines through, attracting and retaining a loyal community.

In essence, conscious social media marketing is about navigating the digital landscape with respect, making a real impact, and practicing authenticity. It's about recognizing social media not just as marketing channels, but as platforms for connection, contribution, and consciousness-raising.

Chapter 4: Self-Assessment Quiz

How would you describe the role of social media in your marketing strategy?

- Vital for connecting with and understanding the audience
- Mostly for promotional activities
- A necessary evil
- Not sure

Which of the following best describes your approach to maintaining authenticity in social media marketing?

- Ensuring that promotional content aligns with the brand's values and mission
- Posting content that is likely to receive maximum engagement, regardless of its alignment with the brand
- A balance of both
- Not sure

How would you rate your understanding of the dynamics of digital relationships in social media marketing?

- Excellent
- Good
- Fair
- Poor

Do you agree that social media can help in developing a conscious connection with your audience?

- Yes
- No
- Unsure

What role does empathy play in your social media marketing strategy?

- It's central to understanding and connecting with the audience
- It's considered but not a priority
- It's rarely considered
- It's not considered at all

In the context of social media marketing, what does 'Satya' (truthfulness) mean to you?

- Transparency in brand communications
- Authentic engagement with the audience
- Both A and B
- None of the above

CHAPTER 5

CONTENT CREATION: THE DIGITAL SUTRA

"Content is not just information; it's a digital sutra, whispering wisdom into the ears of the receptive."

5.1 Storytelling as Sacred Ritual

In many spiritual traditions, storytelling is a sacred ritual. It's a way to convey wisdom, inspire transformation, and build connections. Similarly, in digital marketing, storytelling is a powerful tool for engaging audiences, sharing brand values, and fostering customer relationships.

Each piece of content you create tells a story. It could be the story of your brand, your customers, your mission, or your products. By infusing your content with narrative elements - characters, conflicts, resolutions - you captivate your audience, evoke emotions, and inspire actions.

As you create content, approach storytelling as a sacred ritual. Be conscious of the stories you're telling, the messages you're conveying, the impact you're creating. Craft each story with care, reverence, and authenticity.

5.2 The Power of Resonance: Frequency and Virality

In the realm of energy, resonance occurs when two entities vibrate at the same frequency, creating a powerful amplification. In the realm of digital marketing, resonance occurs when your content deeply aligns with your audience's values, interests, or aspirations.

When content resonates, it strikes a chord in your audience's hearts. They feel seen, understood, connected. They are more likely to engage with your content, share it with others, and act upon its call-to-action. This is the secret behind 'viral' content - content that resonates so deeply that it spreads rapidly across the digital landscape.

As a marketer, strive to create content that resonates, not just content that sells. Tune into your audience's frequency. Understand their dreams, their struggles, their journey. Then, create content that reflects and honors their experiences.

5.3 Content Altruism: Sharing as a Form of Giving

In spiritual practice, giving is a form of service, a way to contribute to the well-being of others. In content marketing, sharing valuable content is a form of giving. It's a way to serve your audience, contribute to their knowledge, and enhance their lives.

When you create content with an altruistic intent, your primary aim is not to sell, but to serve. You focus on providing value - solving problems, answering questions, offering insights. This creates a sense of goodwill and trust among your audience. They appreciate your service, remember your generosity, and often reciprocate with loyalty, advocacy, or purchase.

Thus, the art of content creation becomes a digital sutra - a guideline for creating meaningful, resonant, and altruistic content. It invites you to approach content creation as a spiritual practice, where storytelling is a ritual, resonance is a goal, and sharing is a form of giving.

Chapter 5: Self-Assessment Quiz

How do you approach storytelling in your content creation process?

- I use it as a fundamental framework for all content
- I use it occasionally to make some content pieces more engaging
- I rarely consider storytelling
- I don't see the relevance of storytelling in content creation

What role does resonance play in your content creation strategy?

- It's crucial to create content that resonates with my audience
- It's important but not a priority
- It's rarely considered
- It's not considered at all

In your opinion, does your content act as a form of giving to your audience?

- Yes, it provides value and meets their needs
- Only if it directly promotes my products/services
- No, it's more about promoting my brand
- Unsure

How do you understand virality in the context of content creation?

- It's about creating content that is shareable and resonates with a wide audience
- It's about creating content that triggers an immediate reaction, positive or negative
- It's just a matter of luck
- Unsure

• Content Creation: The Digital Sutra •

What are your main goals when creating content for your digital marketing strategy?

- To inform, engage, and provide value to my audience
- To promote my products/services and boost sales
- To gain visibility and increase brand awareness
- All of the above

CHAPTER 6

CUSTOMER ENGAGEMENT: THE DANCE OF INTERACTION

"In the dance of interaction, we move to the rhythm of empathy, compassion, and genuine understanding."

6.1 Mindful Listening: The Art of Customer Response

Just as a spiritual practitioner seeks to cultivate mindfulness and listen deeply to the whispers of their soul, a digital marketer must strive to listen to their customers with full presence and empathy. This mindful listening involves paying attention to comments, messages, reviews, and other forms of customer feedback, and responding in a thoughtful, respectful manner.

Listening to customers isn't just about hearing their words; it's about understanding their sentiments, their unspoken needs, their underlying concerns. It's about validating their experiences, appreciating their perspectives, and considering their input when making decisions or improvements. This mindful listening fosters a deeper connection with your customers, making them feel heard, valued, and respected.

6.2 Serving as a Digital Yogi: Customer Service with Compassion

In the path of yoga, service is an expression of compassion, a way to alleviate suffering and enhance well-being. In the realm of digital marketing, customer service is a form of service that aims to resolve issues, answer questions, and improve the customer experience.

Serving as a digital yogi involves approaching customer service with a compassionate heart. It's about understanding your customers' frustrations, showing empathy for their struggles, and doing your best to provide solutions or support. It also involves maintaining a calm, patient demeanor, even in the face of anger or criticism.

When you serve your customers with compassion, you not only resolve their immediate issues, but also create a positive impression that enhances their overall relationship with your brand.

6.3 Constructive Conversations: Moving Beyond Negative Feedback

Negative feedback can be a challenging aspect of customer engagement. However, just as spiritual practitioners view adversity as a catalyst for growth, digital marketers can view negative feedback as an opportunity for learning and improvement.

Constructive conversations involve responding to negative feedback with grace and openness. It's about acknowledging the customer's dissatisfaction, apologizing for any inconvenience caused, and addressing the issue in a constructive manner. This might involve offering a solution, making a correction, or implementing a change based on the feedback received.

Instead of seeing negative feedback as a threat, view it as a guiding light, illuminating areas where your products, services, or practices could be improved. In this way, negative feedback becomes a springboard for positive change, contributing to the evolution and enhancement of your brand.

In essence, customer engagement is a dance of interaction, where mindful listening, compassionate service, and constructive conversations guide the steps. As you engage with your customers, approach the dance with grace, empathy, and a spirit of continuous learning.

Chapter 6: Self-Assessment Quiz

How would you describe your approach to customer engagement?

- It's a dynamic, ongoing process that's crucial to my marketing strategy
- It's a necessary part of the business, but not a priority
- It's an afterthought once a sale is made
- Unsure

How do you respond to negative feedback from customers?

- I view it as an opportunity to improve and make things right
- I defend my product/service, as it's important to maintain our image
- I ignore it, as you can't please everyone
- Unsure

What role does active listening play in your customer engagement strategy?

- It's a cornerstone of understanding and serving our customers better
- It's important but not a priority
- It's rarely considered
- It's not considered at all

Do you practice compassion in your customer service?

- Yes, understanding and empathy are crucial in all customer interactions
- Occasionally, depending on the situation
- Rarely, it's more about resolving issues quickly
- Unsure

What's your approach to handling customer complaints or dissatisfaction?

- I try to understand their issue and work towards a solution together
- I offer them compensation to make up for their dissatisfaction
- I adhere strictly to our company's policies, regardless of the customer's feelings
- Unsure

CHAPTER 7

DATA AND ANALYTICS: THE INSIGHT MEDITATION

"Data is not just numbers; it's a mirror reflecting the reality of our actions, guiding our steps on the path to insight."

7.1 Data: The Divine Mirror

In the realm of spiritual practice, meditation is used as a tool for self-reflection, a means of looking deeply into the nature of one's existence. In the realm of digital marketing, data serves a similar purpose. It offers a mirror that reflects the realities of your marketing efforts, the behaviors of your customers, the dynamics of the marketplace.

Data provides objective, quantitative insights about your audience demographics, their engagement patterns, their conversion rates, and more. It reveals what's working in your marketing strategy and what needs improvement. Like a mirror, it shows things as they are, without distortion or bias.

Approach data with the mindfulness of a meditator. Be open to its revelations, be curious about its implications, be diligent in its collection and analysis.

7.2 Wisdom in Numbers: Interpreting Analytics

Analytics is the practice of turning raw data into meaningful insights, much like the process of meditation transforms raw experiences into wisdom. It involves identifying patterns, making correlations, and drawing conclusions from your data.

Interpreting analytics requires a deep understanding of your marketing goals, your audience's journey, and your campaign metrics. It involves asking insightful questions, making informed hypotheses, testing different variables, and learning from the results.

Analytics provides a roadmap for decision-making. It guides your marketing strategies, your content creation, your customer engagement efforts. As you dive into the sea of numbers, seek the wisdom hidden within. Let it illuminate your path, inform your actions, and enhance your effectiveness.

7.3 Forecasting: The Power of Predictive Insight

Forecasting is an advanced aspect of data analytics. It involves using past and present data to predict future trends, behaviors, or outcomes. Just like a spiritual practitioner uses insight meditation to foresee the consequences of their actions, a digital marketer uses forecasting to anticipate the results of their strategies.

Forecasting enables you to be proactive rather than reactive. It helps you prepare for upcoming opportunities or challenges, optimize your resources, and stay ahead of the curve. It also helps you set realistic goals, manage expectations, and measure progress more accurately.

However, remember that forecasts are not guarantees. They are estimations based on current data and patterns. As such, they should be used as a guiding light, not an infallible oracle.

In essence, data and analytics serve as the insight meditation of digital marketing. They provide a mirror for self-reflection, a tool for gaining wisdom, and a means for predictive insight. As you engage with data and analytics, approach them with a meditator's mindfulness, curiosity, and openness to learning.

Chapter 7: Self-Assessment Quiz

How would you describe your relationship with data in your marketing efforts?

- I regularly collect and analyze data to guide my strategies
- I use data occasionally when I remember or have time
- I collect data but often feel overwhelmed about analyzing it
- I don't collect or use data

Do you use analytics to forecast future trends in your market?

- Yes, predictive insights are key to staying competitive
- Sometimes, when I have the resources to do so
- Rarely, it feels too speculative
- No, I prefer to react to changes as they occur

How do you feel about the phrase 'Data is the divine mirror'?

- I agree, data provides objective insights that help improve my marketing
- I partially agree, data is useful but can be misleading
- I don't agree, data feels too cold and impersonal for marketing
- Unsure

How often do you update your analytics tools or methods?

- Regularly, to ensure I have the most accurate and insightful data
- Occasionally, when I come across a new tool or method I find interesting
- Rarely, it's too time-consuming to learn new systems
- Never, I'm comfortable with the tools and methods I currently use

■ Data and Analytics: The Insight Meditation ■

Do you use data to understand your audience's needs and tailor your content?

- Yes, data-driven personalization is key in my strategy
- Sometimes, if the data is straightforward and easy to implement
- Rarely, I usually go with my gut feeling about what the audience wants
- No, I stick to a generic approach for all audiences

CHAPTER 8

EVOLVING THROUGH THE ERAS: FROM TRADITIONAL TO DIGITAL MARKETING

"Embracing change, we evolve from the cocoon of traditional marketing into the vast, vibrant landscape of digital connection."

8.1 The Shift: Transformation towards New Media

Just as all things in life undergo cycles of birth, growth, and transformation, so too has the field of marketing evolved over time. Traditional marketing channels such as print media, billboards, radio, and television have given way to a new age of digital media that includes search engines, social media, email marketing, and more.

This shift towards digital media has expanded the possibilities of marketing. It has enabled marketers to reach a global audience, to target more precisely, to measure results more accurately, to interact with customers more directly. It's akin to a spiritual awakening, where one transcends the limitations of the physical world and enters a realm of infinite potential.

As you navigate this transformation, be open to the new possibilities, be agile in your strategies, be innovative in your methods. But also remember that at the core, marketing remains the same - a means to connect, communicate, and serve your audience.

8.2 Lessons from the Past: Holding onto Ethical Roots

While the mediums of marketing have changed, the ethical roots of the practice must remain intact. Traditional marketing has taught us the importance of honesty, respect for the customer, quality of products or services, and social responsibility. These principles should not be discarded in the digital era; instead, they should form the foundation of our digital marketing practices.

In the fast-paced, result-driven realm of digital marketing, it's easy to lose sight of these ethical roots. The pressure to increase reach, generate leads, or drive conversions can lead to tactics that compromise integrity or exploit vulnerabilities. But remember that, just as a tree without roots cannot stand, marketing without ethics cannot sustain.

8.3 Embracing Change: The Impermanence of Marketing Trends

The shift from traditional to digital marketing is a testament to the impermanence of marketing trends. What's popular or effective today may not be so tomorrow. New platforms, technologies, algorithms, and consumer behaviors constantly reshape the marketing landscape.

Embracing change is an essential skill for modern marketers. It requires staying updated with industry trends, learning new tools and techniques, adapting to changing customer behaviors, and being willing to let go of outdated practices. It's much like the spiritual practice of non-attachment, where one flows with the currents of life without clinging to the past or resisting the future.

As you evolve through the eras of marketing, hold onto the lessons from the past, embrace the changes of the present, and be open to the possibilities of the future. Remember that marketing, at its heart, is not about selling products or services, but about serving people and adding value to their lives.

Chapter 8: Self-Assessment Quiz

How do you feel about the shift from traditional to digital marketing?

- Excited, it opens up new opportunities for reaching and engaging with customers
- A little overwhelmed, but I see the potential benefits
- Reluctant, I prefer traditional marketing methods
- Resistant, I don't see the value in digital marketing

What role does traditional marketing still play in your strategies?

- It forms the basis of my strategies, which I supplement with digital methods
- It has equal importance with digital methods
- I mainly use digital methods, but still incorporate some traditional ones
- I have completely transitioned to digital marketing

How do you react to changes in marketing trends?

- I eagerly adopt new trends and adapt my strategies to fit them
- I cautiously assess new trends before deciding to incorporate them
- I usually stick to tried-and-true methods and am slow to adopt new trends
- I don't pay attention to trends, preferring to do things my own way

Evolving through the Eras: From Traditional to Digital Marketing

How would you describe your marketing strategy?

- Always changing and evolving with the times
- Generally stable, but I incorporate changes as needed
- Mostly the same as it's always been, with only minor changes over time
- Exactly the same as when I started, I don't believe in changing a winning formula

Do you believe in the impermanence of marketing trends?

- Yes, change is the only constant in marketing
- Partly, while some trends come and go, others have lasting impact
- No, I believe once a marketing method is proven, it will always work
- Unsure

CHAPTER 9

BRAND KARMA: SOWING THE SEEDS FOR LONG TERM SUCCESS

"What we sow in our brand today will bloom in the hearts of our audience tomorrow. Each action is a seed sown into the fertile field of the marketplace."

9.1 The Ethics of Branding: Truthfulness and Transparency

In the realm of karma, every action generates a consequence. Similarly, in the world of branding, every decision you make, every message you put out, every experience you create has an impact on your brand's reputation and success.

To sow the seeds for long-term success, brands must adhere to the principles of truthfulness and transparency. This involves being honest about your products or services, your processes, your intentions. It's about being transparent with your customers, your stakeholders, your team.

Truthfulness and transparency build trust, credibility, and loyalty among your audience. They differentiate you from brands that rely on manipulation or deception. They align your brand with the values of integrity, authenticity, and respect, creating positive brand karma that attracts long-term success.

9.2 Cultivating a Conscious Brand: Social Responsibility and Sustainability

A conscious brand, much like a conscious individual, is aware of its impact on the world and strives to make a positive difference. It goes beyond profit-driven objectives and embraces a broader mission that contributes to social good, environmental sustainability, or global harmony.

Cultivating a conscious brand involves practicing social responsibility - addressing societal issues, supporting worthy causes, respecting human rights. It involves embracing sustainability - conserving resources, reducing waste, promoting ecological health.

A conscious brand creates a ripple effect of positivity in the world. It inspires others to act responsibly, it helps solve global problems, it sets a benchmark for ethical business. And in return, it earns the goodwill, support, and loyalty of customers who value purpose over profit.

9.3 The Brand Life Cycle: Birth, Growth, Transformation, Rebirth

Just as beings go through cycles of birth, growth, transformation, and rebirth, so do brands. A brand is born with an idea, grows with strategic marketing, transforms with changing times, and experiences rebirth with innovation or rebranding.

Throughout this life cycle, the brand's essence - its purpose, values, promise - remains consistent. But its expression - its products, campaigns, experiences - evolves in response to market trends, customer preferences, technological advancements.

Navigating the brand life cycle requires adaptability, resilience, and foresight. It involves knowing when to hold on to tradition and when to embrace change. It involves learning from failures, celebrating successes, and continually striving to enhance the brand's value and impact.

In essence, brand karma is the energy your brand creates through its ethical practices, conscious initiatives, and evolutionary journey. It's the legacy your brand leaves in the hearts of your audience and the imprint it makes on the world. As you cultivate your brand karma, remember that what you sow is what you reap. So, sow with care, integrity, and a vision for long-term success.

Chapter 9: Self-Assessment Quiz

How would you describe your brand's commitment to ethics and transparency?

- It is a core part of our brand's identity and mission
- We try to maintain ethical practices but have room for improvement
- Ethics and transparency are not a major focus for us
- We have not yet considered these aspects

What role does social responsibility play in your brand strategy?

- We incorporate social responsibility in every aspect of our brand
- We have some initiatives focused on social responsibility
- We do not currently prioritize social responsibility
- We have not considered the role of social responsibility

How do you approach the concept of brand life cycle?

- We believe in continuous evolution and transformation for success
- We focus on maintaining a stable brand image with minor changes as needed
- We have not yet considered the life cycle of our brand
- We do not believe in changing our brand once it has been established

How do you manage your brand's reputation in terms of truthfulness and transparency?

- We actively promote transparency and truthfulness in all our activities
- We strive to be truthful and transparent but have encountered challenges
- We are not always able to be as transparent as we would like
- Transparency and truthfulness are not a focus for us

How do you view your brand's impact on society and the environment?

- We consciously strive to have a positive impact and reduce any negative effects
- We have taken some steps to reduce negative impact, but there is more to do
- We do not currently consider our impact on society and the environment
- We have not yet considered this aspect

CHAPTER 10

MARKETING NIRVANA: CREATING ENLIGHTENED CAMPAIGNS

"In marketing nirvana, every campaign becomes a melody of purpose and profit, resonating in the symphony of mutual growth."

10.1 Defining Success: Profits and Purpose

Just as nirvana in spiritual philosophy refers to the ultimate state of liberation and enlightenment, marketing nirvana represents the attainment of the highest form of success - a harmonious blend of profits and purpose.

Defining success in the realm of enlightened marketing isn't solely about the materialistic yardstick of profits, market shares, or conversion rates. It's about aligning these financial indicators with a higher purpose, which could be creating value for customers, contributing to society, promoting sustainability, or transforming an industry.

This dual-focused approach to success ensures your marketing efforts are not just profitable, but also purposeful. It ensures that your marketing not only sustains your business but also makes a meaningful impact in the world.

10.2 Beyond ROI: The Holistic Impact of Marketing

ROI, or return on investment, is a traditional measure of marketing success. However, in the pursuit of marketing nirvana, one must look beyond ROI and consider the holistic impact of marketing.

This involves assessing how your marketing efforts impact various stakeholders, including customers, employees, communities, and the environment. It involves evaluating how your marketing contributes to broader goals such as customer satisfaction, brand reputation, social impact, and sustainability.

Holistic impact assessment requires a shift from short-term, transactional thinking to long-term, transformational thinking. It requires a shift from narrow, self-centered objectives to broader, collective objectives. It's about creating marketing that doesn't just drive sales, but drives positive change.

10.3 Manifesting Abundance: A Path to Sustainable Success

Manifesting abundance is about cultivating an attitude of generosity, gratitude, and growth in your marketing practices. It's about viewing success not as a finite resource to be competed for, but as an infinite energy to be shared and multiplied.

This involves practicing generosity - providing valuable content, offering exceptional service, going the extra mile for your customers. It involves practicing gratitude - appreciating your customers, celebrating your successes, acknowledging your growth opportunities. It involves practicing growth - learning from your failures, embracing change, striving for continuous improvement.

Manifesting abundance creates a cycle of positivity that attracts more success. It fosters a mindset of plenty, which counters fear-based marketing tactics and promotes a more inclusive, compassionate, and sustainable approach to success.

In essence, marketing nirvana is about transcending conventional paradigms of success and embracing a more enlightened, holistic, and sustainable approach to marketing. As you create your marketing campaigns, strive for this higher state of consciousness. Align your actions with your highest values, assess your impact in a holistic way, and manifest abundance in all you do.

Chapter 10: Self-Assessment Quiz

How do you define success in your marketing campaigns?

- We aim for both profits and a broader positive impact
- We primarily focus on profits but consider other factors
- We primarily focus on impact but also need to ensure profitability
- We have not clearly defined success for our campaigns

What role does ROI play in your campaign strategy?

- It's an important metric, but we also consider non-financial impact
- ROI is our primary measure of campaign success
- We focus more on the impact of the campaign than on ROI
- We do not measure ROI in our campaigns

How do you approach the concept of sustainable success in your campaigns?

- We aim for long-term impact and sustainability in all our campaigns
- We try to balance short-term gains with long-term sustainability
- We mostly focus on achieving immediate results
- We have not considered sustainable success in our campaigns

How do you measure the holistic impact of your marketing?

- We use a range of metrics to understand the wide-reaching effects of our campaigns
- We try to assess holistic impact but find it challenging

- We focus mainly on direct results and have not considered wider impact
- We do not know how to measure the holistic impact of our campaigns

What practices do you follow to ensure your campaigns are aligned with your brand's larger purpose?

- All our campaigns are designed to resonate with our brand's purpose
- Some campaigns align with our purpose; others are more profit-oriented
- We do not actively align our campaigns with our brand's purpose
- We have not defined our brand's larger purpose

AFTERWORD: THE JOURNEY CONTINUES: MARKETING AS A PATH TO ENLIGHTENMENT

> *"The journey of marketing is a path towards enlightenment, where success is not a destination but an ongoing dance of growth, learning, and connection."*

▪ Afterword: The Journey Continues: Marketing as a Path to Enlightenment ▪

As we come to the conclusion of this spiritual exploration of marketing, let us remember that the journey does not end here. The practices, principles, and perspectives shared in this book are not definitive rules or final destinations but signposts and waypoints on an ongoing journey. A journey of learning, growth, and transformation. A journey towards marketing enlightenment.

In this journey, marketing becomes more than a profession or a business strategy. It becomes a path of self-discovery and self-transcendence. It becomes a medium to express your creativity, a platform to share your wisdom, a tool to serve your audience, a force to shape the world.

As you walk this path, you learn to see marketing not as a game of numbers, but as a dance of relationships. Not as a battle for attention, but as a quest for connection. Not as a race for profits, but as a pursuit of purpose. Not as a struggle for control, but as a surrender to service. You begin to see marketing not as an act of selling, but as an art of giving.

This transformative vision of marketing invites you to infuse your work with a deeper sense of meaning, authenticity, and impact. It challenges you to move beyond conventional marketing paradigms and embrace a more holistic, mindful, and enlightened approach. It inspires you to elevate your marketing from a mundane task to a spiritual practice.

As you integrate these teachings into your marketing practices, remember that progress is often gradual and subtle. There may be moments of clarity and inspiration, and there may be periods of confusion and frustration. There may be times when you feel aligned and empowered, and there may be times when you feel lost and overwhelmed. But that's all part of the journey. The key is to stay committed, stay open, stay humble, and keep walking.

Afterword: The Journey Continues: Marketing as a Path to Enlightenment

And remember, this journey is not a solitary endeavor. It's a collective expedition. We are all in this together - marketers, customers, businesses, societies, the planet. As we engage in this journey, let's support each other, learn from each other, grow with each other. Let's create a marketing culture that is not only effective and innovative but also ethical, conscious, and compassionate.

As we step into the future, let us harness the power of marketing to not just sell products or services, but to tell stories, spread ideas, foster relationships, build communities, solve problems, inspire changes, and make a positive difference in the world.

May your journey towards marketing enlightenment be fulfilling, fruitful, and enlightening. May your marketing create value, make an impact, and serve a higher purpose. May your marketing reflect your truth, resonate with your audience, and contribute to the well-being of all.

And so, the journey continues. Marketing as a path to enlightenment. The path is long, the path is vast, but the path is beautiful. Onward, dear reader, to a brighter, kinder, wiser world. Let the journey continue.

In service,

– **Jayadev K T**

APPENDICES

APPENDIX A: MARKETING MANTRAS FOR DAILY PRACTICE

Integrity Mantra: "My marketing is a reflection of my truth, and I honor this truth with authenticity and consistency."

Service Mantra: "I am not just selling products or services; I am serving the needs, desires, and dreams of my audience."

Connection Mantra: "In every interaction, I seek to build relationships, foster trust, and create meaningful connections."

Learning Mantra: "Each marketing challenge is an opportunity to learn, grow, and evolve."

Gratitude Mantra: "I am grateful for the customers who trust my brand, the team that supports my vision, and the journey that shapes my growth."

Generosity Mantra: "My marketing is an act of giving – giving value, giving inspiration, giving solutions."

Impact Mantra: "Beyond profits and ROI, I strive to make a positive impact on people, communities, and the planet."

Appendix A: Marketing Mantras for Daily Practice

Abundance Mantra: "I approach marketing with an abundance mindset, recognizing the infinite potential for success, growth, and contribution."

Mindfulness Mantra: "I stay mindful in my marketing practices, paying attention to my intentions, actions, and their impact."

Enlightenment Mantra: "My marketing journey is a path to enlightenment, leading me to higher wisdom, deeper understanding, and broader perspectives."

APPENDIX B: MARKETING ETHICS CODE

Honesty: We commit to truthfulness in all our marketing messages, promises, and practices.

Transparency: We commit to openness about our processes, policies, and practices.

Respect: We commit to respecting the rights, values, and cultural diversity of our audience.

Fairness: We commit to fairness in competition, pricing, and customer treatment.

Responsibility: We commit to social responsibility, environmental sustainability, and corporate citizenship.

Privacy: We commit to protecting the privacy and data security of our customers.

Non-exploitation: We commit to avoid exploiting vulnerable groups or capitalizing on harmful trends.

Sustainability: We commit to sustainable practices in our operations, sourcing, and packaging.

Quality: We commit to providing high-quality products or services that enhance the well-being of our customers.

Continuous Improvement: We commit to continuous learning, improvement, and innovation in our marketing practices.

APPENDIX C: SUGGESTED READING AND RESOURCES

- "Conscious Capitalism: Liberating the Heroic Spirit of Business" by John Mackey and Rajendra Sisodia
- "The Power of Now: A Guide to Spiritual Enlightenment" by Eckhart Tolle
- "The Art of SEO: Mastering Search Engine Optimization" by Eric Enge, Stephan Spencer, and Jessie Stricchiola
- Tools from The Strategizer "https://www.strategyzer.com/"
- "Contagious: How to Build Word of Mouth in the Digital Age" by Jonah Berger
- "Made to Stick: Why Some Ideas Survive and Others Die" by Chip Heath and Dan Heath
- "Karma" by Sadhguru Jaggi Vasudev
- "SPIN selling" Book by Neil Rackham
- Harvard Business Review's "Marketing and Sales" section: For insightful articles and case studies on marketing trends and practices.
- "The Monk Who Sold His Ferrari" by Robin Sharma
- "You Can Win: A Step by Step Tool for Top Achievers" by Shiv Khera
- "Life's Amazing Secrets" by Gaur Gopal Das - Gaur Gopal Das,
- "The Habit of Winning" by Prakash Iyer
- "Stay Hungry Stay Foolish" by Rashmi Bansal
- "Who Will Cry When You Die?" by Robin Sharma

GLOSSARY OF TERMS

Digital Marketing and Spirituality Combined

1. **Attraction Marketing:** A marketing strategy that draws customers to a brand through the creation of valuable, relatable content. In spiritual terms, it's akin to the law of attraction, manifesting customers through positive marketing actions.
2. **Brand Karma:** The notion that the actions of a brand, either positive or negative, will eventually return to it in kind. It reflects the spiritual principle of karma, suggesting that what a brand 'gives out' will ultimately come back to it.
3. **Conscious Marketing:** A marketing approach that prioritizes transparency, authenticity, and social responsibility. This approach mirrors spiritual principles of consciousness and mindfulness, advocating for thoughtful, purposeful actions.
4. **Digital Dharma:** The ethical path in digital marketing, guided by principles of truthfulness, non-harm, and service to the customer. The term 'Dharma' in spirituality refers to the moral and ethical duties one must follow.
5. **Enlightenment Marketing:** The ultimate goal in spiritual marketing, where marketing actions are driven by a higher purpose and universal values. It mirrors the spiritual concept of 'enlightenment', representing a state of ultimate wisdom and liberation.
6. **Marketing Mantra:** A phrase or statement repeated frequently to guide and inspire marketing actions. This reflects the spiritual practice of chanting mantras to focus the mind and align with certain energies.

Glossary of Terms

7. **Marketing Nirvana:** The state of achieving ultimate success in marketing that balances both profit and purpose. It's derived from the Buddhist concept of 'Nirvana', symbolizing the highest state of enlightenment and liberation from suffering.
8. **Marketing Yogi:** A marketer who applies spiritual wisdom and practices to their marketing endeavors, balancing the pursuit of business objectives with a commitment to serving customers and society.
9. **Mindful Marketing:** The practice of applying mindfulness – focused, non-judgmental awareness of the present moment – in marketing decisions and actions. It encourages a careful consideration of the impacts of marketing activities.
10. **Sacred Storytelling:** The practice of using stories in marketing that resonate deeply with the audience, touching upon their emotions, values, and aspirations. It mirrors the spiritual tradition of sharing sacred stories or parables to convey profound truths.
11. **SEO as a Path:** Viewing Search Engine Optimization not just as a tool for better website ranking, but as a path to truth and transparency, ensuring that valuable, relevant content reaches those who seek it.
12. **Social Mandala:** A term depicting the intricate network of relationships in social media, reflecting the interconnectedness and interdependence of all beings. The term 'Mandala' in spirituality symbolizes the cosmic diagram that represents wholeness and unity.
13. **Virality and Resonance:** The phenomenon where a piece of content spreads rapidly online due to its resonance with the audience. It echoes the spiritual concept of 'resonance', the harmonious connection or alignment with certain energies or vibrations.